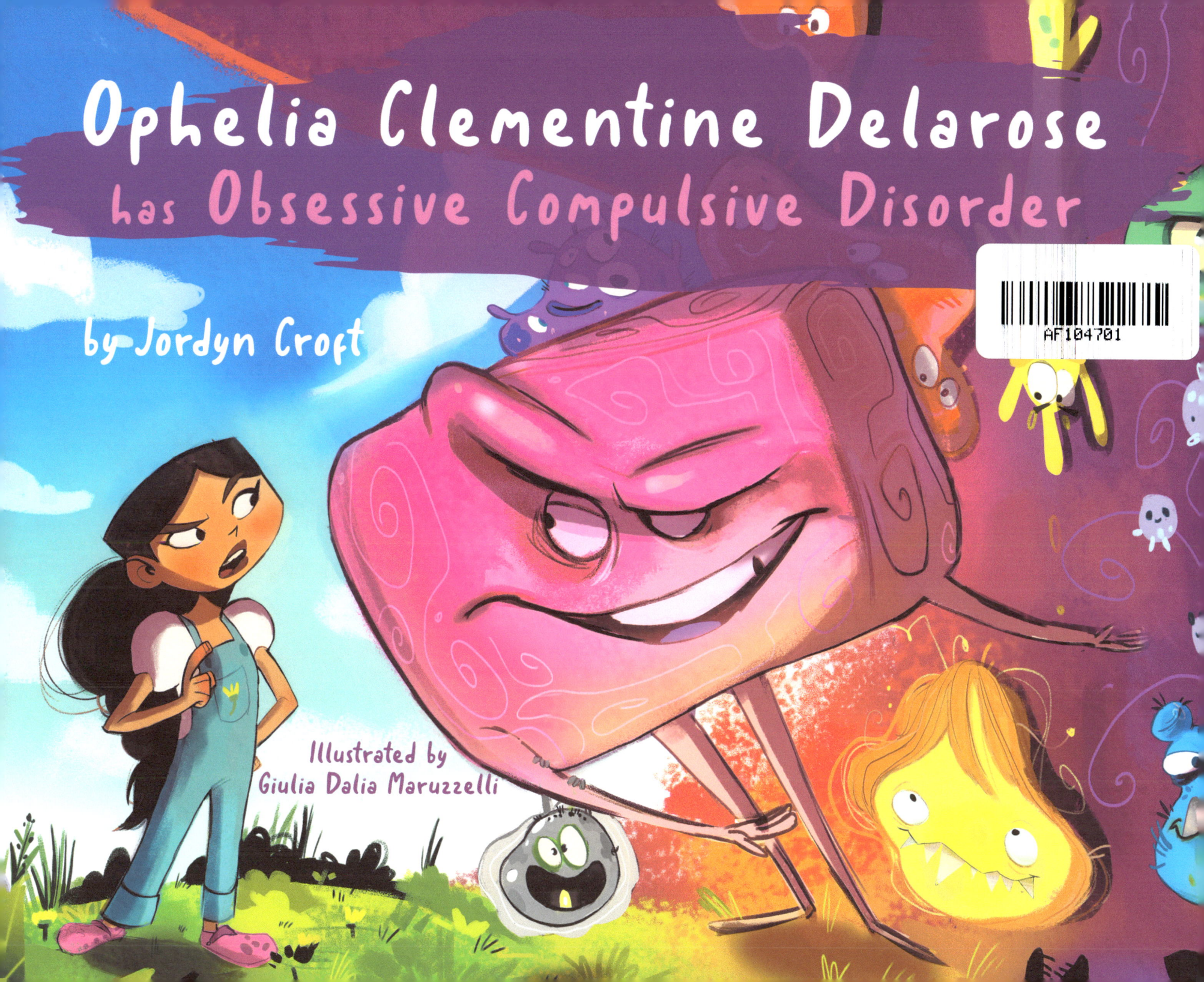

Ophelia Clementine Delarose
has Obsessive Compulsive Disorder

by Jordyn Croft

Illustrated by
Giulia Dalia Maruzzelli

Ophelia Clementine Delarose has Obsessive Compulsive Disorder
Copyright © 2021 by Jordyn Croft

All rights reserved. No part of this publication may be reproduced, distributed, or transmitted in any form or by any means, including photocopying, recording, or other electronic or mechanical methods, without the prior written permission of the author, except in the case of brief quotations embodied in critical reviews and certain other non-commercial uses permitted by copyright law.

Tellwell Talent
www.tellwell.ca

ISBN
978-0-2288-6242-0 (Hardcover)
978-0-2288-6241-3 (Paperback)

Dedication:

For every young person who needs the reminder that they are stronger than their tricky brain.

Acknowledgements:

Thank you to all the people in my life that have been a part of my mental health journey, and those who have been involved with the production of this incredibly special book.

Ophelia Clementine Delarose dropped her orange coconut donut on the floor.

Her brain tries to trick her into thinking that she has to leave it there or else she'll get germs all over her hands.

She tells her brain no, and puts the donut in the garbage where it belongs.

Ophelia Clementine Delarose will only say odd numbers while counting down in math class.

Her brain tries to trick her into thinking that this pattern will keep her family safe.

She tells her brain no, and practices counting properly.

Ophelia Clementine Delarose went to the outdoor community garden to feed the deer.

Her brain tries to trick her into thinking that she must go back home right away to wash up.

She tells her brain no, and enjoys her time outside.

Ophelia Clementine Delarose has to open and close the dishwasher to help her little brother.

Her brain tries to trick her into thinking that she needs to wear gloves for protection.

She tells her brain no, and decides the handle is perfectly safe to touch.

Ophelia Clementine Delarose was told by her parents to only wear her Crocs downstairs.

Her brain tries to trick her into thinking that she can't let her feet touch the stairs without them.

She tells her brain no, and leaves her shoes by the front door.

Ophelia Clementine Delarose isn't supposed to overfeed her cat named Delilah.

Her brain tries to trick her into thinking that she must measure the cup of food 3 times before putting it in the bowl.

She tells her brain no, and measures the cup just once.

Ophelia Clementine Delarose felt one of her elbows touch Camilla's dress at school.

Her brain tries to trick her into thinking that she needs to have a shower to feel clean again.

She tells her brain no, and moves forward with her day.

Ophelia Clementine Delarose has Obsessive Compulsive Disorder.

Her brain tries to trick her into thinking that she'll feel unbelievably uncomfortable until she does what it tells her to do.

She tells her brain no, and continues to use her inner strength to stand up against the intrusive thoughts.

www.ingramcontent.com/pod-product-compliance
Lightning Source LLC
LaVergne TN
LVHW071733060526
838200LV00031B/481